To Seek God's Face

Vivian Kearney

ISBN-13: 978-1-63065-149-7

PUKIYARI PUBLISHERS
www.pukiyari.com

*Thanks for their wonderful help
to dear husband Milo,
our daughter Kathleen and her family,
our son Sean and his family
and our ever patient editor, Ani Palacios*

Dedicated to all of us of a certain (third) age, helpers,
near ones and mentors, now and passed

Table of Contents

True Clues, Good Connections 151

Seekers

Journey Companions

Thou, O Lord
Hast forever planned
To walk on the earth
With us

So we were made
To be bipeds, balancing
On legs, feet and toes

Just as amazing
Especially for babies
As infant birds
Learning to fly

Please stay with us
Help us balance and move
In our wheelchairs too

Seeking Each Other

Seeking, we are
Crying to the vaults of heaven
– Where art Thou, dost Thou hear
Our prayers, suffering, needs and fears?

God is
Calling down the corridors of time
 – Where are you? Do you know
I have formed you yesterday
I see you tomorrow
I am waiting to give you mercies

Then let us faithfully forever
Convene together

Accepting Favors

We all have our bags
And baggage

How love works to pry
These away

From our dusty thoughts

Help we should accept
When forgiving charity
Doesn't fit into

Ever heavy, ever needy
Unfair survivor guilt
Luggage

Border Lands

There is still a desert on both sides
Of the now bustling border cities
Once cocooned, sleepy

There are ever veiled lands
Under an unknown sun
On both sides

Of this teeming, rushing existence
Given by our invisible Creator
Of this life-sized planet

To help us walk
Into Heaven's eternity

Looking for Cleopatra's Tomb

Too much mortal sadness
From too many eons back
On quests to discover deep shafts
For tombs, near temples past

One day we'll find her bones
Molecules of her once soul home
But when and where will we see
Our way out from tunnels of melancholy?

To Comfort Cries

A baby's lonely yearnings
Left unattended

Can cry beyond
Milestones of years

All the medications, dedications
By the adult self
Cannot fully dissuade
Those moans away

Grown perceptions
Cannot deeply persuade
The still desperate infant heart

That only God's grace
Can fully comfort from above

With His all-encompassing
Son-brought love

Rescued Journey

Leapfrogging ideas
From watching, talking, reading
Give bounces to hopes
That threatened to be crushed
By tired, solitary cynicism

And once more, thank God
We can see connections, plan projects
Resume seeking His face
With calmer, happier steps
And pilgrimage promises can be kept

Hiking Guides

Dear Abba, thank-you for
So many mentoring hints

That, as hiking guides, advise
At just the right moments

And for those helpful angels
Carrying pinpoints of light
Like stars at night

Lost Meditations

So many trails lost
I believed there would be time
To rediscover, to recreate
Out of the day's rhymes

For written word journeys
To beautiful coves
Where God keeps ships ready
For missions, visions and roles

Generalizing From Particulars

Generally, we can see
The heart has two sides
And the soul has its shadows
Nations travail
Through their own woes

Though God highlights
Marvels that can shine
With maps of philosophies, psychologies
Biblical histories inspirational

While His angels like to illuminate
Particulars

Such as
Cornflower blue dawns
Purple weed florets
Sweet individuals
Wondrous

Statements

Statements only God can say:
About His identity
About His work

— I am
— I am good
— It is finished

We can just wander, pondering
Who our genes say we really are
With some help from the likes of
Ancestor.com

We can't state we're totally good
Since we each have our shadow side

We can't really feel we're finished
With a mission, ministry, project, journey

Although we are encouraged
To bestir our hearts and souls
And keep on keeping on

Exile, Loss and Recovery – Genesis 2:19, 3:23;

Luke 15:4-32

The first loss ever biblical
Was the expulsion from Eden
Door shut to conversations spiritual
With the Creator, Who so wanted
To discuss names and explorations

Now, whenever we lose track
Of memories, dimes, clothes or papers or people
Our hearts hurt, our minds desperately
Search hidden corners, sweep houses and when
They're found, we feel found again

Reading A Similar Seeker

A valley poet
Born nineteen thirteen

She couldn't
Have had a more contrasting back story
For her poems

But wait...
These were from the same town, college
Where she and I studied and taught

We might have met... or not
Our life journeys were parallel

In some ways
We write as similar seekers
Though in another style
At a different time

Thank You

These, your poems
Souvenirs from your journey

Deliver pictures
Worth a thousand words
From eternity

Called

One was humorously greeted as
The Yiddish Mark Twain

The other, conversely, addressed as
The gentile Sholom Aleichem

Both called to take
Divergent yet comparable
Light-hearted literary paths

To seek God's smiling face

Isaiah 6

The higher they fly
Our deeper thoughts
The more they can stay
On mountain tops

Lord, help us, our lands, earth
And families so loved
May all our cares and hopes
Look for Thee above

Orbits

With our twirling, whirling personal planets
Orbiting around each other –
Soul mates, parents, children, families
Sisters, brothers, friends and neighbors
Tied by gravity, we spheres dance seemingly freely
In our own biomes, lit by lovely moons

But forces from somewhere make us move away
To galaxies unknown, far from previous homes
Moving to new music, for a while in fun styles
Though the left-behind, nostalgia-clouded worlds
Sigh and cry without efficacious words

Convoluted Stories

Convoluted stories
Half-begun, labyrinthian,
Scattered pages of our lives

Only God can turn
And find a pressed flower
Of a soul poem inside

That abides
To be revived
In His garden kingdom

Questions

Blame and Redemption – John 9:1-6

Who sinned, my parents or I?
And who is responsible
For my neuroses unreasonable?

Who is to blame for the Holocaust?
What people in which generations
Of enemy nations?

And where shall we cast the God-given lifelines
Of forgiveness? To whom should we
Talk about His salvation?

Let us keep doing the work for the One Who sent us
When night comes He will be the light
To guide us through labyrinths of hidden histories
And we will be redeemed in His forgiving sight

Painful Balance in Nature

Lord, Thou couldst create by evolution
Just as Thou keepest us in place by gravity
Yet how couldst Thou also be kind, have mercy
With such a painful balance of survival?

Instead of fierce competition,
Couldn't we all get along?
Dying peacefully of old age as said Isaiah
Lion and lamb could praise Thee with hallelujahs
Wild creatures and children
Could worship Thee with song

As domesticated animals, when treated kindly
Can serve with pure, true devotion
Couldn't all be in peaceful symbiotic relation?
To witness Thou art God of many mercies

Will we ever know or understand?
Are pain and suffering tests or workouts of faith
That we should still minister thankfully
That we should still reach for Thy hand

Part Driver?

You think
You're the full-time driver
Of your soul

Things will prove different
Like objects
They hide away
In dancing spaces

Just when you thought
You could help God
By getting at least a little
Disciplined, alert
Organized and mindful

So where does that leave
Us, Lord?

If Not on a Lone Island

What is freedom?
Is it a fantasy, red herring or reality
To do everything on our own, individually?

Is that even possible
At this non-lone-island place
In this post-cave age?

Is it freedom to escape the constraints
Of civilization, society
That we depend on to be
Protected culturally, medically?

Does it put us in a different bind
Since nature, human weaknesses are not totally kind
And easily, with gravity, self-reliance unwinds

Almost Too Much to Keep Track

Difficulties falling asleep
When questions weep

Does abundant nature
Destroy and / or provide cures?

How to outlast this pandemic
Can we plead with God's Holy Spirit?

When will God's loving grace
Show His benevolent caring face?

Can we choose selfless, wise beliefs
To get political, economic, health relief?

Will we the next days, decades, centuries
Glorify and honor God, walk in His mercies?

Faith

Is it a ship
That we can hop on
And be carried, communally
Or individually
To Eden now, heaven later

Is it a road
That we can explore
Sometimes leading us linearly
Or often meandering

Is it a light
To seize, to keep
In the mind's eye
Pulsating
Through forests of thought

Is it a leap
Into the unknowable
Does it need to burn bridges
Of previous learning
Of words of reason

Is it a temple or dwelling
Built or natural
Kept clean and bright
Where God would like to talk

Is it a shield
To protect against
Arrows of cynicism
Slings of fortune

Is it a vision
Paradigming your life
Landscaping your stay
Here and forever

Is it a language
Without worldly words
That communes
In a quiet spirit room

Is it a will
To be as positive as possible
To blanket against
Cold's icy threats

Is it a grace
Offered to all
Accepted by some
While others question

Is it a call
To show mercy, respectfully
Or to be judgmentally
Righteous, triumphant and cured

Is it an offering
Of our hopes
That we can give
To Thee, Lord

Into Thy invisible hands
To the music of Thy heartbeat
And evidences of
Thy love

Although Questions Still Echo

Where does the light start?
When is the music heard?
What information will be welcomed?
What silence can be understood?
Where should the race be run?
What award should be won?
What I-Thou conversation?
How soon begun?

Much To Be Done

To be told, to be read
To be advised, to be held
To be imagined, to be analyzed
To be taught, to be apprized

Will we take the faith road shown?
Will we reap what we have sewn?
Will we dance with the red-gold sun forever?
Will we be redeemed to talk with our Savior

About how to flag our own train
How to be helpful while in pain
How to achieve something good with our tries
Yet only God can lead us to decisions wise

Meetings

Who would meet whom then?
What would they say
In the lands above the sky
While lilting music plays

Who meets whom here
On what iceberg-tipped course?
May the ships we build for our thoughts
Inclusive benevolence endorse

Was There Ever?

When did our stay on God's good earth
Ever look promising to the Creator
O fellow humans?

Was there ever a decade when
We were kind to all, including the soil
And not in food chain competition?

How do we weep for our depredations
Stop treating the planet linearly
While walking a caring road
Seeking God's peaceable kingdom?

So Formed by So Much

Have we, the exiles
Been so formed

Not only by determining genes
By our names given by family's whims or constants
By first languages

But also by our habits ingrained
By our cultural geography
By the physical landscapes of our beginnings

Desert or mountains, trees, rivers, skies
Quality of surrounding light
Golden, pale blue, dusty, silver

By our old technology
And ever resonating
Favorite mood music

That
Our expressions and questions
Our walks and our talks
Vocabulary, intonation, conversations

Mark us
Even now
That we've travelled
Out of the early niche
In space and/or time

Obviously strangers
In a strange land

Lost and Searching

Like lost characters
In an unfinished novel
We asked pleadingly

—Are you our Messiah?
The one to lead us against Rome
Into the promised kingdom
Of a free Israel?

Or should we
Look for another?

—No, answered Jesus
The search stops with Me
For I am
The Way, yet also
The Light at the end of your road

Firstly

What will happen at first
To all our questions
When we're in heaven?

We'll be so bedazzled
We will sing amazed
Hallelujahs

While hopefully also hearing
God's compassionate answers

Surprize! He is Here

Who is this who comes riding
Into the city, into our traditions and souls
On the back of a donkey with her foal
Into our Jerusalem of gold?

It is Jesus, the prophet of Nazareth
The son of Joseph, the carpenter from Galilee
His father is descended from David's family
But why is Jesus overturning our tables of money?

Who are you, Lord? I can already guess
Thou art my King and our Lord of rests
Who suffered on the cross to tear the veils
From our hearts
And a more loving spirit to our baffled world impart

Shouldn't This Temple Last Forever?

Matthew 18:21, 22; Matthew 24:2

—But our temple is so beautiful, imposing
Rabbi Yeshua, why do you foresee
That this holy place will be demolished
Doesn't such a structure witness God's glory?

When shall these things be?
How before and then should we live?
Just another question more, *Rabbeinu*
How many times should we forgive?

—Temples are mired in traditions and time
Forgiveness should be endless
Love Me, love your neighbors as yourselves
And you and many will be blessed

Did You Cry?

– Jesus, did you cry
At Gethsemane
For all the wrongs
We did to Thee?

– Jesus, did you cry
At Calvary
For our cruelties
And tragedies?

– I cried in the garden
I bled on the cross
For promises unkept
For lives that were lost

For coldness of hearts
For jealousies and contentions
But I did visit to find and lead
Past, present and future
People to salvation

To Seek God's Face

Why do I want to seek God's face?
To thank Him personally
For the flowers of wonder, gifts of grace, and
O for all the love

Journey

Setting Out

Into the light waves
Oceans of the day

Learning the names
Via internet information

Of the exquisite
Consecutive

Seventy some
Blue colors

Of the skies
Displayed

You Will Need Them

From previous tragic histories, fallen strongholds
Take some beams, rocks, iron, mortar, coal

To build bridges with Me,
To pass over fearsome seas

Then you can communicate your encouragement
With loved ones, acquaintances, neighbors, friends

New Year's Resolutions 2020 (Written Pre-Covid)

Look back
Look forward
Janus-like
This January

Remember the mentors
The people, the places of before
Realize how the arc of your life
Was shaped, is ever unfolding

Ruminate, not too compulsively
About twenty-twenty and beyond
Hope for continued opportunities
For old-new languages, inspiring songs

Unwrap the gift of the present
Meditatively, gratefully
Smell the roses yet to bloom
Walk on waters trustfully

I'm Indebted to You

Dear Abba, Milo, family
Rescuers, mentors
Helpers not a few

You don't owe me anything
Though you mean so much to me
I don't own you

If we traverse valleys of despond
Lord, keep us from bitterly feeling
More is due

Let us love God morning and evening
Even in twilight's garden
Shrouding the dawn's dew

To Be Arranged

Elderhood
Denial or embracing
Trying to outrace
Aging's foreshadowing
Unfair and too early

Starting to realize
(It's about time)
That seconds are
Made of diamonds,
Hours of pearls

To be arranged
Creatively, artistically
Moments are not just sand
To let slip through
A careless hand

At the Point

I'm at the point where
Medicines taste better than food
Shared silence better than symphonies
Rest better than multi-levelled adventures
Meditational paths better than cultural outings
And I don't seem to have a working role to uphold

But wait, what about caretaking's missions
Or housekeeping's tracks
Or translation's boat, or writing's airplane
Or reading's train or media's car
Or albums to arrange, biographies …
Even echoes can provide a stand

So, chin up, keep calm, carry on
This home, computer await a few efforts
This stage offers its own ministering gifts
Let's see what God will sift

Slower Journey

En la tercera edad
(In the third age)
D'un certain age
(Of a certain age)

Now is the time, the place
In any language
To celebrate aging

Slower steps
Encouraging appreciation
Maps on skin
Changeable
Silver highlights
Landing on sparse hair
Far-sighted long-term memory
To make up for short-term gaps
Mellowed feelings
Nuanced opinions
Appreciation of all generations'
Journeys and stages

Learning much about the body
Through illnesses, pains
Meeting medicines, nurses, doctors, procedures

Needing locomotion, transportation help
Nourished by simple foods
Returning to humble dependence

Beholding elderhood's mirror image
… Long ago childhood

Bookended Life

Beginning of life
Finale of life
Bookends for our
Journeys and stories

Signal stay, thank God
Enjoy this present stage
Of intense caring, caregiving

With daily treasures
More beautiful than diamonds
That love brings

Two Roads

Freedom! Scream parties of corporate needs
But without responsibilities, who will heed
Necessities for individuals, families, Creation,
Health, nourishment, transportation, education

Good governance, not less, can help
Better lives, equality, justice to all fairly dealt
Whereas some people's choices about exclusive rights
Leave too many with freedom from
Shelter, health, protection and light

Tips for the Journey

Sunglasses
Preferably rosy colored
Provide air conditioning
For the eyes

Twinkling bubble baths
Suggest poems
For the morning's preparations
And the day's ride

Lengthy or short prayers
Send telegrams
From the hopeful soul
To God on high

Do the Next Thing – After Elisabeth Elliot

We think we
Know and can do
What the next thing is
To attend to

But planned paths
Metamorphize
Become as narrow as twigs, then
Turn into multi-colored
Multi-shaped shards
Of a kaleidoscope

And, with a twist
Of the viewing glass
Show another pattern
Needing different mindfulness

With calls, doctors' visits, prescriptions
With conditions changing
Even objects becoming uncooperative
And we still don't discern
What would be best managed
And in what order

Lord, please give us good courage, wisdom
Strength, hope and faith for
Continuing our lives' missions
Our days' journeys
Step by next step
For Thee

Ruth's Journey – Ruth 1:1-4:22

– Dear mother-in-law, Naomi
Don't go angrily alone
Your God will be my God
Just let me stay with you
In fellowship true

– Dear daughter-in-law, Ruth
I don't know how we'll travel
Though God has a golden sunrise place
And He weaves our lives with His love
From above with divine grace

Beyond boundaries and our fortress mentalities
Past pride of nations, shelter and traditions
Shine the constant hopes of the promised land
Where we can thrive, holding God's hand

I can't conceive whom you might meet
And I don't have anything to give you
Yet my name changed from Marah, the bitter one
Because of your friendship

And we'll share circumstances, family customs
Walking together
With and to God's salvation

Aliyah – Going Up to Live in Israel,

After _Israel Is Real_ by Rich Cohen

Israel is real
And so are the ghosts
Who made _aliyah_ after death
To welcome their living relatives

In the one and only
Historical and holy
Beloved old-new land
Of their dreams

After a Storm in San Antonio

After their cousins
With their grey, billowing forms
Had warned us about storms

The sunnier new clouds
All yellow, pink and mauve
Float innocently by

Parading and smiling
Their painted blessings
From the pale blue sky

September Storms

September storms still grumbling
After flashes and thunders through
San Antonio's evening and night
What can homeless ones do in their plight?

What are their journeys under furies
Of weather and uncaring legislators
What can we do to relieve their adversity?
God, please send everyone
Help, guidance and charity

Barred Babies

The children, the babies, the fetuses
Not allowed to discover
The roses, the poems
On life's roads

May they be tenderly welcomed
By our eternal Father
And His cherishing angels
With eternal love
Into heavenly abodes above

Carpeted Steps

More than soft – actually plush
Green weedy grass carpet
Waves with a slight breeze
Smiles with starry flowered
Summer's welcome for my footsteps

Once Closer

Dunes and seaweeds
Shells and trails

We strolled along
Not at the same time, mostly

Each with our own families
Though we shared that scenery
The air, the sand and the sea
Knowledgeably

Then we headed for the hills
And you stayed
On the frontier near the beach

And now
It's not so easy to reach
Beyond the divide

Transport and Port

Poems swim
In sweet, peaceful waters
Of existence slowly
Savoring their aqua molecules

Gap Time

Why not just
Give the sunny shadow
Of this afternoon's
Slowing, perplexing
Gap time

To God also
While waiting

For those
Surprisingly quick minutes
Next to the supper hour

Then relax in our easy chairs
As we're informed, entertained
Together with this evening's
Television offerings

Spring Stage

Chrysalis this life
Until we get eternal wings
We're awkward over here

Ignoring A Southwest Summer

Below the too bright summer sky
Among tired parched plants

Cicadas shriek their warnings
Of unresolved global warming

While willingly oblivious
Not going anywhere
We seek shelter

In artificiality's air conditioning

Pre-Thanksgiving

Showers of gold and loveliness
Leaves fall without a sound

Yet, let thankful songs abound
In every season with reasons all around

Winter Decorations

Is your life
A Christmas tree

With all its blessings
As souvenir ornaments

Heading towards a star

Saved Trip

For choice, Lord, Thou hast ever been for choice
As Thou hast chosen us, we should choose Thee
And walk heedfully through situations thick and thin
Avoiding pitfalls of pride and viruses therein

For life, Lord, Thou hast ever been for life
Not wanting that we perish in darkness and strife
But that we sing forever in sweet harmony
With angels and saints glad praises to Thee

Watery Meditations

The accidentally
Spilled shampoo forms
Outlines of soapy foam

The warm bath water speaks
Of a forgotten stay in an
Unknown wartime womb

Did I smile or cry
At my birth and soon sing
Polish songs in ghetto rooms?

Hugs

The lost child that I once was
In a Polish orphanage
Just flashed by as a ghost
Across memory horizons

Smiled and asked when
And where are we going
What will I be at seventy-nine
And who will care for me

The wife, mother, grandmother, senior,
Retiree that I am now, in San Antonio
Answers and reminds me every day
Reasons to be amazed and thankful

For God's unimagined love
For my dear soul mate
For scarcely hoped for
Family blessings

To look back, reassure
And hug that little lost child

One Lost Sheep – Luke 15:4,5

Jesus looked for one lost sheep
The one who was differently driven
He could leave the others for a while
Those who tracked the fields and miles

But the little lost one wandered
Not knowing the way from flowers fair
A little ADD, maybe Asperger's
But on Jesus' shoulders he was a-okay

Balance of Wills, Wheel of Fortune

We had thought
It all hung in the balance of the will
That most of our decisions and path choices
Helped by fortune's wheel
Delicately turned on a dime

To take courses at McGill
To change into an 11 o'clock class
Where we heard in our hearts
God's marriage plan

Then led to take Spanish
To have children in South Texas
To join a little Baptist church
And myriad other choices

But Thou, o Lord
While we were deciding
Didst secretly create a path

Surely Thou settest us on the way
To Thy marvelous light
And wonderful conversations

Please do so also
For the blessings
Of all others

Strolling, Walking, Resting

Strolling in the snowy heaven
Of seeing your eyes, your steps
Beside me, in Montreal
You were an angel of change, of travel

And now we still hold hands, resting
At home, sheltered from southwestern droughts
And late summer's thunderstorms

Walking yet together, dearest Milo
With souls always intertwined
Under the setting sun

Morning (Thy Word is a Lamp Unto My Feet –

Psalm 119:105)

Morning cedes its stars
The sky turns lighter blue
By degrees

As if God turns on a lamp
Dispensationally, considerately
For our time-bound minds

That need scheduling hints
Prodding, telling us to
Jump on the day's train

Slowly, though
With all due haste
By the light of His word

Journeys – Biblical Leitmotif

Interesting leitmotif that
To accompany our quests
From beginning to end
Genesis to Revelation

The Bible gives us
Among other lessons, themes,
Histories and good news

Stories of national and individual journeys
And their unforgettable moments

Phases, junctures, points
In humanity's
Spiritual odyssey

Feared Horizons

Ne Me Quitte Pas – **Don't Leave Me**

Proceeding to an Italian restaurant
A planned celebration designation
To meet with family

You walk ahead a few steps
As, OCD-like, I hang back
To recheck the car door

So far, so soon the distance
Gives me a second's jolt
A heart wrench, *verklemt*

Until you turn around
And I catch up, erasing space
And we're together again

Road Markers

As an amateur home nurse for beloved
Fine, necessary objects I find
For this private, makeshift hospital
For these caregiving needs
Physical, emotional, educational, spiritual

Even while
Events threaten to become resonant markers
To be noted and managed. Still,
I try to negotiate every step with the Father
Eternal within each state

With its
Fine, necessary objectives
Though measurements may be pushed aside
Let's consider the many wonders and signs
That we can forever with God abide

Ask Not – After John Donne

Ask not
For whom the red and blue lights
Of the ambulance flash

They blink for you
Announcing your impoverishment
A disappeared sphere here

A warning
For every one of us

And our postponed fears

Metamorphized Soul

A golden-hued flower
Was called to fly
Into the blue yonder

So it turned into
A floating, fluttering
Yellow butterfly

Visited and conferred with
Its erstwhile cohorts
In their shared language

Who were still rooted
Communing with the earth
But now learning about
The bright, high sky

Preparations

Lord, we may be leaving
Soon or very soon
Or in a decade or two

What will we be placing
In a time-capsuled present
For family, for posterity

It is a good though depressing thing
To contemplate and wrap up this life
As far as able, neatly
Or at least slightly

This wonderful journey given
With known and unknown graces
Love, angels, mercies, children, friends
Rescues and charities

Lord, please give us time, energy
To prepare, to pray
For salvation, blessings,
Protection, ministries

For those staying, for those already left
Let us all forever walk close to Thee

And Counting – Hopefully

Why did you think the moments,
Of these sixty-some years together
(And counting, hopefully)
Would last forever?

As fragile pink and aqua bubbles
Floating on waters of the present and past
They return too soon to rivers of time

And yet, why do you think
They completely disappear?
Their memory molecules are everywhere
Ageless witnesses, happy to share

Our lives through
Pencil, photos, books, computer and song
Lending near trees and flowers a voice
To portray love, to hum hallelujahs

And through lonely tears
With Thy mentorship, comfort
Worship Thee, God
Eternally

We, the Dinosaurs

We would laugh at them
O how much fun it was
To remark how little they knew
About food, long distance calls
Franchises, clothes, cars
The English language
New media

Now it's we, the dinosaurs of this century
Who don't know much about
High-tech terms, communications
Wi-Fi, platforms
With portable computers and their apps availability

And we wonder how and when
Life passed us by

Erased

Marvelous how
After cleaning, dusting
Spots and stains disappear
From surfaces, announcing innocently
There's nothing to see here

Whereas
It's discouraging how
Some politicians launder and spin sad facts
Sacrificing truth to win media games
Lying – There's nothing to see here

Slippage

Bridges over rivers
Sturdy enough to dance on
Valiantly supporting
Any number of rushing cars
Even through mighty winds
Stronger than predicted

Though, for lack of caution,
Materials carelessly pinched
Some structures fell
As shown on TV
More fragile it seems
Than rope crossings in the Andes

Bothersome bite on leg scabbed
Then mindlessly scratched twice
Bandage left too long, infected

And this caregiving occupation
Jeopardized, can slip, unfortunately
And transform instantly
To a different kind of life

Lord, please cure wounds
Bridges, souls and bodies
Caught in dissonance

Be persuaded and strengthened
Cared for, led and mended
By Thy Holy, healing Spirit

O Retirement

I thought the lovely, chatty muse
Would visit more often
Poems would range farther, deeper
With more words at my fingertips
Time lending endless cues

But that muse and her diligent relations
Have been packing up
And seem more than ready
To travel away
Into unknown, feared horizons

Hide and Seek

How infinitely many thoughts
Kind, wise, planning, spiritual

Have been lost and now wander
As unattainable stars

Winking their diamond hints
Of hide and seek lights

In the blue velvet night

One of the Locks is Time

Though,
As light shut in a box
Or behind a door

Can still escape
Its confining edges, locks, corners

So love
Can shine through, above and around
Fortresses of determinism
Bolted by time

Imagine then
What God's Holy Loving Spirit

Can do
For this seemingly sentenced planet

Fear of Shade

Good deeds, wise care
Why are these so difficult
To play forward or to share?

Do they throw shade
On those helped or noticing, implying
Their less admirable weaknesses, traits?

Or – is it our own fears
Of continuing on the road
To meet our Father Savior

The only holy and truly good One
Throwing us into the shade
Of our weaknesses, failures?

Yet we are told, yet we need
To do good deeds, *mitzvot*
For others as we do for ourselves

With courage and God's love
Offered to all from above

Some Goals Change, Some Hopes Fade

Treading in place diligently
Trying to avoid impending pitfalls
Worries multiply and some goals fade
Varied Covids, literal and allegorical
Threaten lives, personal and social

Yet let us carry on with faith and devotion
Giving fears, goals and hopes to Thee, God
Who most importantly, understandingly
Offers love, comfort, redemption and salvation

Help Us, Lord

The things we need to do
We have no strength, Lord

The progressive aging
We can't turn back, Lord

The mistakes, medicinal quandaries
We fear the outcomes, Lord

And miss the serotonin, energy
To face problems, to resolve conundrums

Individual, national, historical, global

Lord, we need more of Thy love
Please help, o God

Be Heartened, O My Soul –

After Mark 8:23-26, John 9:6-41

He
Put teardrops in my eyes
And I do see
Amazedly

He
Took my thorns of bitterness
And gave me many bouquets
Of grace

He
Rewove the frayed threads
Of circumstances
And helped me braid
Thankful poems

He
Leads us, waits for us truly
No matter how unruly
Fears want to be

Remember
Be heartened
O my soul
And neighbors all

You Know

Faces of fear, why are you hovering near?
Love is forever and God is here
He counts your hair and redeems each tear
You know you've received His help year by year

Prayers and Promises

Often

Often in church
And sometimes out
We can sense
God thinking of us

And we wonder
What walks He's preparing
Reviewing prayers and promises
For our alpine talks

Through Stages

Youth's mountains
Old age's valleys
Teen's volcanos
Middle age's plateaus

Not to criticize heartfelt prayers
Nor judge topographies and stages
Since we all need God's help terrains to cross
And ask for the way when we get lost

Water Wings

The poems that I send you
Are water wings

So you can walk on
The seas of your story

Towards Me

Exile's Prayer –

After *Lost in Translation* by Eva Hoffman

Worrisome the worries
Resonating the conundrums
Melancholy the shades of nostalgia
Changed from one hour to the next

Like hiking clothes being tried
In preparation for the day's pilgrimage
In a quest for symbolism's cathedral
That could answer questions of first identity

The exile's path keeps threatening
To lose its surety with those changing stages
Through this new land's shifting cultural terrain
Evoking cries – Where is my *shtetl*?

Of before, of now, of the future
Whose tradition can envelope me
And where can I sing the lyrics
That I'm told to discover

Who Knows

There are
Many thousand truths
In millions of books
But I can't read them all

Please let me rest in Thy arms, Lord
Knowing Thou knowest everything
And canst teach the hushed stars
To sing

Healing

Lord, please help all nurses
And give permanent care
To those who donate tiptoe support
Plus all critical and micro-news
Of yearned recovery share

Lord please support each medical helper
So intimately involved
With others' health
Then dropped quickly
From patients' lives restored

Let the healers also know
They are permanently
Beloved by Thee
Their mission reintegrated
Constantly

Once in Heaven

Once in heaven, may it be
Neighbors far and near continue
Past positives joyfully

Language learners will chat around tables
Line dancers will move gracefully
Parishioners will pray devotedly
Sent angels will keep mentoring
Poets will new psalms sing

And even here, in frequent valleys of fear
May we thank God He is always near

Passages

Having in your heart
Oceans wide and deep
Having in your soul
Promises to keep

Let God travel with you
Even this passage steep
For God's love and healing
Ever pray and weep

Soothed

The stars cry too
Since their cradles
In the cosmos
Will become red, then
Blue dwarves
Then can disappear
While the heavens themselves
Leave for parts unknown

Yet the night vibes still soothe
The worried mornings
And prayers for this planet,
For Creation
Find their way to God's home

Letters and Lines of Alliteration

Solitude sent for souls especially
To search the serendipitous seas
To meander among meanings and moons
To find the forgiving, faithful Father

Even when away from the warmth of church worship
Hoping the Holy Healer will still hold our hands
Although belief can blunder into doubting bogs
Letters and lines longingly sing lilting lullabies

Accept sweet steps into surrendering sleep
Hum helpful tunes, ponder shimmering shadows
Looking to the Lord Who leads lovingly
Sing thankful psalms for His blessings and mercy

Little Faith

Little faith
You can do it
You can walk over water
Little faith
God will heal you
You must set out and try

To find His kind kingdom
To seek His holy grail
Many will be the wise signs
On the given trail

His love will astound you
His grace will surround
Take a little step into love
Little faith
And He will your name renew

Let Us Find, Dear Lord

Comfort in smaller spaces
Away from past exhilarating races

For our microcosms also hold
Marvels wonderful to behold

When we spend hours more slowly
We can contemplate weeds and pebbles lowly

While reviewing blessings of previous years
Giving thanks for people dear

And prepare for heaven's meetings
God, loved ones and mentors greeting

Asking for forgiveness, redemption
Healing for all and eternal salvation

So Long, Backpacks

Carrying for so long
Backpacks of dusty thoughts
Together with ever new abrasive sands,
Unpearlized as yet

And those heavy grains trickle
Out of the accumulated baggage
Turning into quicksands
Of sorrows, pains and regrets

That we want to
Regather, repack and recount
But they have their own force fields…
Lord Jesus, please don't let

Them overcome us,
Loved ones. Give us strength
To leave those laden backpacks
To rally thankfulness and prayers
For everyone – unknown or met

Wishes

What I would wish
For past die-hard skeptics
Who expired saying
Creation created itself

Would be a beautiful heaven
An eye-opening college above
Much like the garden of Eden
Where God would discuss

How and why the cosmos
Came into surprized existence
Through slow evolution
Or miraculously quickly

The Creator explaining the journey
Of each nucleus, cell, organism
Every planet, galaxy, nebula
So we could sing together
Glad hallelujahs

At the End of the Day

At the end of the day, Lord
Help us return all to Thee
With gratitude and praise

Leaving pride aside
For naught gets done
By our strength, on our own

And let us leave works haplessly undone
Also in Thy hands as we understand
Only Thou canst complete and mend

Then, let that be true
At the start of the day too

With Yeshua – Matthew 19:16-26

Change – said Yeshua
To the young man seeking
A rabbi's advice about
How to obtain everlasting life

– Oh, but I'm good
I own and gladly use
This wealth well
And have dutifully
Observed the laws
You mentioned

Yet still
Tell me the secret
Of the key to eternity
Just don't command me
To give away my goods, my money

–You see – said Yeshua
To his *talmidim*
How hard it is
To give up comforts, funded paradigms
On a dime

–Then – worried the students
Can anyone be saved?
Can this world
Be regenerated?

Can we witness and work wisely
For Thy new kingdom?

– Humanly, hardly
Said Jesus
Looking at His disciples
Compassionately

Yet all things are possible
With Me

Please Be

Abba, Lord, please lead us to that bridge
Between Thy peace-bringing
Reassuring promises
And our wide-eyed worries
About unfairly heavy gravities

Abba, Lord please be the divine bridge
Linking our life-affirmations, protections
Here on earth

And our prayerful donations
Of all we own
All we owe
All we are
To Thee

Mitzvah, Tikkun Olam – Good Deed,

Saving the World

Because of your *mitzvah*
You helped us feel stronger
Go on a little longer

Because of God's divine *mitzvah* – *tikkun olam*
Promised and given
We can receive salvation

Lord help us
Look everywhere
For chances to share
Thy good news and deeds

Let Us Have, O God

Faith, let us have faith
As we get carried out by tides
That there will be some signs
To accompany our goodbyes
Like Jonah

Hope, let us have hope
That we can build ships
For wondrous, adventurous trips
Of creativity, service and worship
Like Noah

Courage, let us have courage
Over slings of discouragement
To pray for missions lent
To move with God's providence
Like Moses

Wisdom, let us have wisdom
To be guided by His grace
To see each stage as a sweet place
Where we can His message witness
Like Joseph, like Paul

Love, let us have love
Gratefulness instead of regret
Joy with the Holy Spirit
And all to His love commit
Like and with Thee, Lord Jesus

Sometimes, Always

The dimpled clouds will sometimes frown
Dancing trees will sometimes bluster
The peaceable ground will sometimes shake
But I will never leave you nor forsake

Smiling skies will change and threaten
Sweet breezes can gather into storms
Heavy showers will sometimes overwhelm
But I do govern every realm

The saddened tunnel will arrive at a light
The trackless forests may murmur messages
The stranger can change into a lifelong friend
And I am with you in the beginning, middle and end

The lonely road can lead to lovely libraries
The deserted plains to new ministries
The empty hours to precious gifts of time
For prayers, creativity and learning
If you put your hand in Mine

Promises From the Cross

I promise you
That you will be with Me
In paradise

Where there are
No disabilities or fears
Robberies, wrongs or lies

Where people
Are all well-advised
And their lives eternal
Are sweet and beautiful

Where everyone and everything
Is calm, helpful, true, brave
Healthy, wise and joyful

Why not here, Lord?
Why not now?

Please heal our illnesses, disabilities
Deficiencies somehow

Let everyone find
And understand

Thy good news plan
And Thy continuing story

The Truth, the Way and the Light - John 14:6

The way to My house
If you ask Me, you will see
The truth you can depend on
I offer redemption and salvation

Pursuit of selfish happiness
To others' detriment
Is actually the wrong road
I promise you a better goal

The lighted path to lead you onward
To My kingdom of love and kindness
Though it's sometimes hidden here
My word can make helpfully clear

God's Perspective

The bird's eye view
Of humanity
In the Bible

Makes us think
The One Who understands
Must live above our lands

And who would that be
Except God, the Creator Almighty
Perspective Keeper

Tabernacles Here – Matthew 17:4-7

– Dear Teacher
Thanks for appearing
On this mount of Transfiguration

Oh, Rabbi
Let's build some
Tabernacles here
To remember
This wonderful occasion
With Thee

– No need, just listen to Me
Commemorative edifices
Don't always
Have to be built
Here on earth
Those will always be
Sadly temporary

Yet, cheer up
My kingdom can be within you
So that I'll meet with your souls
And talk with you
In your hearts
Wherever you are
Eternally

What is Easier for Jesus – To Forgive or to Heal? –

Matthew 9:1-8

If, Lord, Thou forgivest all
In order to heal all
Then let us pray Thou wouldst
For salvation universalist

True Clues, Good Connections

True Clues

Spiritual quests on musical paths
True clues to be found and cherished
As the soul's treasures and heart's light
Sent from a numinous, intangible height

Words fleeing from fidgeting pencil
Can they write insights by themselves?
Will they bring back spiritual balm
These tired racing thoughts to calm?

Frames of days flipping fast and slow
Into another year's movie reel
Composed and distributed by God, the Director
Who yet lets us drink free will's nectar

Breathtaking Picture of Mount Rainier

Early in the morning
Started the computer
And what did I see on screen?

Soft grey blanket of clouds lifted
And the ringed flowers
Give a vibrantly coral shout-out
To God, their Painter

Deuteronomy 6:4, 5

Love God,
Love your neighbor
As yourselves

To be able, stable
And give care
Wisely

While reaching for
That numinous word
That describes His face

Goodness

Dream

In the backseat
Of a familiar classroom

With a sweet teacher
To whom you didn't have time
To say good-bye
Before she disappeared

And your car in the parking lot
Was safe, but not the trees
Making way for a wider street

Then the flashing word
Does Christ say
You belong or not
To this waking world

House at Night

Flashlight flower on the wall
With three luminous white petals
An eclectic example of a trinity

Reminding me
To think of God, Christ, Holy Spirit
Three in One

Forever shining
Waiting for our walk
With an I-Thou talk

Less Is More

All I need is one pencil to write
Not several

All I need is one orange light
To start warm musings

All I need is some time
To type some lines

All I need is to forgive unknowns
By secretive, rescuing adopters
Easier said than done

Except if helped
By the forgiving
One

Adopted

I was two and a half, not four
I was seven and half, not eight
I spoke Polish, the secret language, fluently
Then why did I forget it immediately?

Did it bother me to be finally told a family secret
That turned out to have many gaps also
I was so brave and blasé about it
Not letting inner earthquake show

Which wasn't really all that surprizing
Rather like new pieces to a still
Unfinished puzzle, for the key parts were taken
To the grave by a very strong will

Did I have the right to ask – I thought not
But did come close to accusations
Yet how could I hurt survivors of horrors when they
Had so carefully built their new-world havens

Then what, Lord, dost Thou want me to do now
Where do those clues and connections lead
With that old document, a retreat, a novel
Encouraging the telling
And not fear the teeth
In that forbidden theme

Blessed Pregnancies

Mijita
I hug your little beige pillow
With its classy cutout patterns
Close to my stomach

As I cuddled you long ago
When I carried you inside

....

Mijito
I remember when
I would open the refrigerator door

How you, a fetus at the time,
Would jump for joy

Evolution of Our Sabal Palm

From its frozen orange colour
Battling a weather challenge wintry

Our sabal palm now greened
Looks like it's trying to be
A Christmas tree

With its present conical shape
Its original trunk ringed
With sprouting fronds

Also a reminder of us, the older generation
And visiting young grandchildren
Playing, dancing around

Pilgrimage

I looked for God
And what did I see
A beautiful, branching tree

I thought about God
And what did I find
Resonating biblical lines

I searched for God
Meanwhile He sent
A loving soul mate, sweet family
Convivial friends

To contemplate nature together
Events, programs, history, and weather

Please God, forever
Here and in heaven much later

Intercessory Prayers

Vaults of overarching
Trees on streets, each
Praying for the house, the people
You shade, protect

For the concerns you discern
Within the human habitat
With your nerve-like branches
And trembling, photo-celled leaves

You were grown by God
Let us be heartened
By your resonating, medicinal
Understanding

Waiting at the Dollar Store

The idea fled
And won't be captured

The muse disappeared
To other islands

The leaves don't know whether
To say their winter goodbyes
Or early spring greetings

Time, my frenemy
Calms with sighs

A breeze pushes the empty swings
Humming a quiet lullaby

Blessings of Advancing Years

Old age's nuancing abilities
To hold two ideas
Two perspectives or more

In your heart, in your head
At the same time
As well as closing many loops
Biographical, historical
By rationally noting
Reviewing your earlier journey's
Once hidden clues

These and so many more
Treasures of advancing years
Sent to give you empathy
With more understanding
Of yourselves and others

So you can walk relieved
Of some distracting conundrums

Into the afternoon
Evening and
The angel-lit night

Food and Aging

Morning
Time to take care
Of your newborn systems

Noon and afternoon's
Table and snacking
Curiosities
May get in the way of
Working abilities

That can continue anyways
Only so far

Evening and night
Time to be more mindful again
With aging's fragilities

Homebound

Our very own
Walden pond
Only here, as we're homebound
Nature peeks into rooms
Through frames of windows

Begging the questions
Where do we come from
Where are we going

Not dust to dust
Rather to and from
Our spiritual home
Heaven's rest

Time, Like a River

Time, like a river
Doesn't wait on you
It's not a servant or pet
It can't really be paused

Except when you
Get lost in the moment
And /or pray
Or write a poem

Clues of Climate Destruction

This morning and often
I wrapped myself into
An ocean-themed bath towel

Hoping I and it
Didn't contribute to harm
Those beautifully pictured
Water creatures

Neat Planet

Abba. as I fold up towels
I think about
How Thou arrangest healthy nature
With divine economy

To clean up
Plus keep beautifully decorated
This neat planet

Smoothed

Shake out the sheets
Folded and crumpled
Once, and they spread almost flat
Twice and they straighten
And smooth out

My life had so many wrinkles
But with many incremental pulls
God ironed the creases
Made it readable, useable
Unfolded out

Home Treasure Hunts

Gratefully exploring
My closet's clothes
Somehow all my favorite colors,
Sizes and styles
From the past

Times when
I could leisurely visit stores
To my curiosity's content
Driven by insistent
Shopaholic habits

That have thankfully disappeared
Since the pandemic
And homebound requirements

Awoke Afresh

—Hello! Said the much-missed key
Winking from a most unlikely
Lost place. I'm not going to tell you how I got here
However, now that you've learned your lesson
Let's just celebrate our reunion

—Hi there! Said the morning clock
Surprizing me with its leniency
Now that you've caught up to me
What will we continue to work together
To glorify God, our mutual Redeemer

—Greetings! Said God, the Counsellor
Now that you're both fully awake
Let Me lighten yesterday's backpacks
And help you, advise you
For this fresh day's journey anew

Pilgrim's Progress Revisited

Thanks opens the doors out of dungeons of bitterness
Where we languish on chairs of torturing rage
Praise tears grim grasses of choking envy
Uncovering sweet roses, rosemary and sage

Prayer unlocks the cage of selfishness
Converting to compassion competitive moods
Humbleness rejects the heavy fare of pride
So we can dance lightly, fed on spiritual foods

Singing exiles lonely night sorrows
Raising palm branches opens our hearts
Appreciation discloses colorful flowers
Ready to cheer with their God-given art

Trust lays siege to the castle of suspicion
Announcing a new reign of faith in the land
Forgiveness banishes the cruel giant, revenge
The clenched fist becomes a helping hand

Repentance leaves self-righteousness behind
Letting God keep accounts and lost souls find
Gratefulness opens our minds to grace from above
Realizing Jesus is the door to God's kingdom of love

Reached

Mountaintop views yesterday
Heady and inspiring Holy Spirit
I'm so ready to revisit

But today is another day
Dazzling in its own way

We Have Been Given

The sun by day
Stars and moonlight by night

Visions' goals by day
Dreams' clues by night

God whispers through silence
And His musical universe

Sparkling with signs and wonders
Communicates His love

God is the *Shomer* - Guard

Abba, Thou art the *Shomer* of the morning
The tenderly paling blues and greys
The awakening symphonies announcing
Yet another miraculous shining day

Abba, Thou art the *Shomer* of noon
The sun telling us to work
Through weather, valleys, marching
In time with Thy calming word

Abba, Thou art the *Shomer* of afternoon
When time runs out of our horizon
Too quickly and we latch on to stuff
That can hide our spiritual mission

Lord, Thou art the *Shomer* of twilight
When veterans of the hours and age
May walk and talk with Thee in the cool
Of eventide, discussing each past stage

Abba, Thou art the *Shomer* of the night
Its neon dreams, streams of unknown consciousness
Thou guidest ships of souls through mysterious waters
Giving our pilgrimages blessed rest

For These and More

For love's caregiving clues still whispering
For families close and neighbors visiting
For friendly phone chats can still have
For mentors past and present still teaching
Thank you Lord

For fun memories still chuckling,
For house still cooperating
For time still accommodating,
For good projects ongoing
For medical professionals,
Medicines, vaccines still helping
For some legislators still respectful, honorable and fair
Thank you Lord

For our journeys continuing
With angels relaying Thy gifts of grace
For Thy natural wonders still inspiring,
For flowers bravely smiling

For Thy answers sooner or later
Addressing our questions
For Thy word ever talking about love,
Redemption and salvation
Thank you Lord

Celebration

Yesterday, Today

Ask me, tell me, soft
What blessings we received, oft
What good God has wrought

John 1: 1-5 – The Light of the World

The light of the world
The message in the word
The peace in the quiet
The love of the Holy Spirit

The footsteps in the sand
The rainbows over dry land
The silver in grey clouds
The wonders all about

The comfort in the talk
The pilgrims on the walk
The beauties of the season
The soul's eternal reasons

To recollect all God's cares, for
He has been with us everywhere

When and Always

When the late afternoon shadows
And sunbeams play on the grass
And highlight the trees with their fleeting goodbyes

Let's celebrate the wonders the good Lord multiplies
And His name forever magnify

Let Us Walk

Beloved, let us walk
You and me
In the garden
By the sea

Let us talk
You and me
Sharing and learning
Constantly

Let us live and love
You and me
Helping one another
Thankfully

Abba, let us celebrate Thy Creation
Thou and us
And how to steward
May we with Thee discuss

Step by Step

Step by step
Dearest friend Milo
We have travelled you and I
Realizing that with
The truth, the way and the light

God is bringing us
Wisely, softly
Back home

To His land of
Multifaceted, divine
Love

Anniversary Song

Dear Milo, when
I looked into your eyes
When we would walk and hold hands
In Montreal's snowy lands
I could hear infinity's call

Dear Milo, whenever
We look at each other now
Tired age melts away
We return to that very first day
And celebrate our anniversary

Practice

Will we wait on tables
Joyously
In God's mansions?

Is it good to listen, write
Meditate, sing and paint
To dispel fears here

To celebrate and practice ministries
For later, when we're together
In heaven's haven

Human Scale

Colors are letters
Paper and canvas
Are one grammar
To recreate on a human scale
God's language and art

On Various Places

I wonder if Martian families
Go touring red sand landmarks merrily
And if moon people enjoy their vacations by
Jumping between craters gleefully

Just as curious that we, earth creatures here
Use holidays to travel, visit, write and discover
This tiny planet, our so-patient home sphere

Stop and Marvel

A tiny pinkish white butterfly
On a minute yellow weed flower
What a sweet
Miniature world of beauty

Through it All

Rejoice!
Through it all
In so many ways
Helping and caregiving

Brings you closer
To each other,
And to God's divine
Provident Holy Spirit

Vivid Too

On the phone,
Dear kids and grandkids,
Staying in this house, we

Ask you where you went
What you did today
How's everything
What you're planning
What's new

Vicariously
Enjoying that trip
Living that journey
Visiting that landscape
With you

At this time, physically
That's all we can do

And those mind excursions
Shared experiences
Are wonderful too

Evidences – I Corinthians 13:1-13

Evidences of God's existence
Radiate through shadows of doubts
Lifting veils of sorrow

Love, truth, beauty, rescues and redemptions
Everyday gifts and miraculous wonders
Especially and best

Love
That shines through
All tests

With Us

Does God
Celebrate with us
During holidays, special events
And lovely days in between

Do we, in trust
Rejoice with Him

Marvelling at His visionary ingenuity

Survivor's Birthday

The true birthday date
That we celebrated
This, my seventy-ninth year
Yesterday

I actually don't know for sure
And why from torn Polish beginnings
Did I seem viable to the war sufferers
And rescue-worthy

We do appreciate, gratefully
That we're all here
Miraculously, on this side
Of life

Thank you dear rescuing Abba

Encouragement

Reaching back, can move forward
From toddlers holding my hand
To reading wonderful birthday words
To recalling heartening times
To a beautiful planter presented
Green and maroon vines intertwined

Birthday gifts that keep giving, reminding
Of the flowing, woven, continuing path
Of family love

A Mother's Influence – by Sean Kearney

Writing, how do I write?
Language, how do I speak?
Teaching, how do I teach?

So much of what I am
Is a reflection of where I'm from

19 Acacia Drive
Homer Hanna High

My mother's son

I and Thou World – After Martin Buber and

Robert Burns

What happens when, surprized
A person comes across another
Going through the rye
Maze of life

As lifetime soulmates introduced
As parents beholding their child

It means being chosen
And choosing to care
Steadily, lovingly

It invites a convivial walk together
Towards the supreme
I-Thou meeting

Even here on earth
With loving caring
All-hearing, all-seeing
God

Drive Down 1-10, Revisiting Brownsville

with Milo and Son Sean

The night upon the flat land
So still, yet breathing its somber words
To the dark sky while we drive by
Its unheeded sighs

The lovely reconstruction of history
In song, poetry, antique restored buildings
Awards to those who worked diligently
To highlight their true border beauty

The manicured campus on the southmost frontier
Some downtown houses repaired, others not
Now tropically multicolored, our old abode
Glimpsed next to nostalgized palm-lined road

The people long prayed for
Suddenly appeared, talkatively
Into reality's frame, then moved as we headed home
To reflections' two dimensions again
A cloud of memories of a day well spent

May God bless all with continued creativity
In the delta valley by the ever-murmuring sea

Revisiting Montreal With Daughter Kathleen

Wanting to share my history,
Our Canadian relatives,
Worlds, places and stages
We plane-hopped to the past

Houses, streets, parks still snow-covered
The university campus where journeys started
An elementary school now much smaller
Once immigrant neighborhood now gentrified

Sparkling subway stops below
And touristed districts above
Visits with welcoming hosts,
Celebrating departed generations
Photos and souvenirs gathered

Then we were time-machined back again
Wondering how it all could have happened
In four lovely short days

Little Miracle Revisited

A toy horse
A plastic, weighted
Palm-sized lost toy horse

A little grandson cried for
Once fifteen years ago
After the family's move, to San Antonio
500 miles away
From his first home

Wait, what?
How did that happen?
We spied it, five hours later
At our new home, transported
On the top of our car

And the boy was very happy
And we were all comforted

Fast forward
One day before his big college move
About two thousand miles away, to British Columbia
After we had discussed
Myriad family memories

The teen rummaged the green room
Of his past sleepovers
And came back with
The very same, long forgotten
Faithful toy horse

Lovely, nostalgic moments
To revisit, to witness together

Think on These Things – Philippians 4:8

The beautiful, the wise, the pure and the kind
Prayers and thanks for those that come to mind

Help us rejoice when God grants petitions
Wonderfully
With the true, the wise, the lovely, the kind
Sent miraculously

Light Restricted, Light Limitless

A small worn-out flashlight
Only lets you see
Restricted narrow spaces
Shadowy individual objects
One at a time

Imagine how
God's own
Limitless light
Helps Him view
The universe with
Each and all particulars
Wholly together

Life Here, Life Eternal

Celebrate the search
Note the clues and connections
Understand the fears

Commemorate the journey
Remember the questions, answers and lessons
Bless God Who grants prayers

As we continue on this life-long pilgrimage
Let's exalt His name at every stage
And meet in Heaven's kingdom eternal

Advent – Celebrating God's Arrival Here

At the end of the day
Let's recount
The infinite reasons
To celebrate Advent

May we discover that God
Seeks and finds us
With His amazing grace
As we seek His face

www.ingramcontent.com/pod-product-compliance
Lightning Source LLC
Chambersburg PA
CBHW051753040426
42446CB00007B/351